EBONY ANGELS

EBONY ANGELS

*A Collection of African-American
Poetry and Prose*

compiled by

FAITH JAYCOX

ILLUSTRATIONS BY TERRANCE CUMMINGS

*Crown Trade Paperbacks
New York*

Published by Crown Trade Paperbacks, Inc., 201 East 5oth Street, New York, New York 10022. Member of the Crown Publishing Group.

Random House, Inc. New York, Toronto, London, Sydney, Auckland

http://www.randomhouse.com/

CROWN TRADE PAPERBACKS and colophon are trademarks of Crown Publishers, Inc.

Printed in the United States of America

Design by Nancy Kenmore
Illustrations by Terrance Cummings

Library of Congress Cataloging-in-Publication Data
Ebony angels: a collection of African-American poetry and prose/ compiled by Faith Jaycox. — 1st paperback ed.
    p.   cm.
Includes index
1. American literature — Afro-American authors. 2. Afro-Americans — Literary collections. 3. American literature — 20th century.
I. Jaycox, Faith.
PS508.N3E26   1996
810.8'0896073 — dc20   96-23381
                            CIP

ISBN 0-517-88746-0

10 9 8 7 6 5 4 3 2 1

First Edition

EDITOR'S NOTE: In spirituals, most dialect spellings have been standardized. In addition, some dialect spellings have been modified for clarity and ease of reading in the folktale "Angels' Wings and Men's Shirts"; Paul Laurence Dunbar's "Banjo Song"; James Edwin Campbell's "When Ol' Sis' Judy Pray"; and Fenton Johnson's "Lif' Up de Spade." In all cases, I have attempted to balance the contemporary reader's need for clarity with respect for the author's desire to capture folk speech.

CONTENTS

Introduction 8

THE POETRY AND PROSE

INTRODUCTION

❁

Angels, it might be said, attended the birth of the African-American literary tradition and have hovered about it ever since. Angels appear in the earliest published poem by an African American, "An Evening Thought" (1761), by Jupiter Hammon, who lived and died a slave. Today, more than two centuries later, they continue to inhabit contemporary works like "Arrival" (1983), by Maya Angelou, whose poetry helped celebrate the inauguration of President Bill Clinton, or "On the Road to Damascus" (1989), by Pulitzer Prize winner and Poet Laureate Rita Dove. During the intervening years, literary angels have appeared in almost every form of African-American writing: autobiography, fiction, folklore, religious and political essays. They have graced joyous spirituals as well as Martin Luther King, Jr.'s heartrending funeral sermon for the children killed in Birmingham in 1968. They have populated humorous folk stories as well as the writing of activist and intellectual W. E. B. Du Bois.

Why, we might ask, have God's messengers and guardian spirits appeared so faithfully in the African-American literary tradition? First, of course, they express a deep religious faith in the greatness of God's power to effect divine purposes. Second, they express an encompassing spirituality that is part of the African heritage. Yet it cannot be denied that the historical experience of African Americans—enslavement, discrimination, injustice—seems to speak more clearly to the power of evil than of good. Because of that experience, in fact, some skeptical observers have questioned the wisdom of focusing on a heavenly world or of emphasizing spiritual life. Both tendencies, these skeptics argue, have interfered with the urgent need to change conditions on earth.

According to the African-American writers included in *Ebony Angels*, however, those who disparage the relevance of religious faith and spirituality to earthly life are unequivocally wrong. In some selections, the role of the angels is to sustain and encourage humans through trying times, reassuring them of divine care. Perhaps more importantly, in many selections, the spiritual perfection of these beings is a literary means of focusing attention on earthly imperfections. The presence of angels in these works subjects the errors of the world's judgment to a higher authority.

Angels derive their meaning and importance from their relationship to the divine. While their primary role is to praise and serve God, they are also God's emissaries. They convey divine truth to human beings who inhabit the fallen, imperfect, and sometimes malevolent world. In the African-American literary tradition, angels are particularly concerned to impart two important truths. The first is that God has created all of humankind in the divine image: race and social station cannot, and do not, determine one's value. The second is that God wants humankind to be—in both earthly and spiritual senses—free.

That human beings are made in the image of God is, of course, an orthodox religious belief. It is important to remember, however, that it is a belief from which some white Americans once sought to exclude black Americans. Almost as soon as the first Africans landed at Jamestown in 1619, they were confronted by the demeaning argument that they lacked individual souls. For African Americans, therefore, every assertion of spirituality was a vigorous denial of the status they had been assigned. Every assertion of spirituality became an assertion of full humanity and a rebuke to those who would deny them equal participation in earthly life. As the colonial poet, and slave, Phillis Wheatley pointedly reminds her readers, even dark-skinned people may "join the angelic train."

During the nineteenth century, autobiography was the most popular form of African-American writing; as the autobiographical selections in *Ebony Angels* show, many believed angels to be a real spiritual presence working in their lives. Both in spiritual autobiographies and in slave narratives, angelic visitors urge autobiographers to recognize the importance of their individual souls to God. To female African-American autobiographers, angels bring the news that gender does not affect their worth in God's eyes. At the same time that these nineteenth-century women struggled with the burdens of slavery or discrimination, they were also defined culturally as innately weak and domestic. Yet the angels who visit future itinerant preachers like Jarena Lee or Julia Foote insist that "womanly" reticence does not excuse them from following God's commands. The angels' message is clear: Black or white, rich or poor, male or female—all have been created in the divine image, and all are of equal value to God.

Closely associated in African-American writing with this message is the idea of freedom. Among the selections included in *Ebony Angels,* freedom might well be termed the controlling metaphor for divine purpose. Without doubt, part of that purpose is freedom from injustice on earth. "Freedom's angel" is a familiar spirit in African-American writing, bringing not only good news to humankind, but joy to those in heaven.

It would be clearly wrong, however, to suggest that earthly freedom is the primary concern of the angels. In traditional religious thought freedom is primarily a spiritual concept, not a physical one; it is a condition defined by salvation. The emphasis on spiritual freedom in the African-American literary tradition is rooted, doubtlessly, in the experience of earthly, physical bondage. Nonetheless, freedom of the spirit is sought, proclaimed, and celebrated in many selections in *Ebony Angels,* including some predating the end of slavery. The long, powerful

tradition of joyous descriptions of Heaven, for example, honors the perfect state of freedom that exists there.

It is the devil's purpose to steal human freedom, both in spiritual and physical senses; not surprisingly, then, African-American writing is also keenly alive to the presence of the fallen angels. "I believe in the devil," W. E. B. Du Bois declares unequivocally. In folk tradition, the characterization of the devil is enriched by the African figure of the trickster. "Old Satan is a liar and he conjure too," as an old spiritual puts it. In religious tradition, Lucifer and his legions are aligned with, if not responsible for, earthly evil as well as spiritual bondage. It is the devil who tries to make autobiographer Jarena Lee doubt her spiritual sanctification, but it is also the devil whom poet Elymas Payson Rogers imagines authoring the Fugitive Slave Law.

Throughout more than two centuries separating Jupiter Hammon's time from our own, the message of the angels in African-American literature has remained unchanged: Human dignity and freedom are the Creator's plan. The authors included in *Ebony Angels* see no conflict between earthly needs and spiritual concerns. The earthly values that they honor have spiritual counterparts in the angels' heavenly truths.

Angels appear in a rich and perhaps surprising variety of African-American writing, as the selections in *Ebony Angels* illustrate. Their subjects vary widely, expressing the different interests, purposes, and experiences of individual authors. Some write freshly and powerfully about major biblical events—the creation of the world, the expulsion from the Garden of Eden, the conversion of Paul, the crucifixion of Christ (the latter unforgettably described in "The Death of Jesus: A Sermon" from Zora Neale Hurston's *Jonah's Gourd Vine*). Some portray meaningful biblical figures: Moses, leading his people out of slavery; Lazarus, raised from the dead to a new life on earth; Jesus, born a poor child, suffering, yet triumphing as King Jesus. Some selections reflect the importance of the church, its rituals, and its ministers in African-American life—and, in the folktale "Angels' Wings and Men's Shirts," the tradition of folk humor that has grown up around them. Another significant group of selections reflects events of African-American history, particularly slavery and, in the twentieth century, the civil rights movement.

Other writers explore the angelic presence in less obvious places—music, for example. "The spirit does not descend without song," says an African proverb, and as the selections in *Ebony Angels* illustrate, a long literary tradition honors the musical talents of the celestial host. Fenton Johnson, for example, imagines Israfel, the angel of music, as Lazarus's guide through Hell. To some, the angelic talent is associated with African-American singers, particularly women. Robert Hayden writes a moving memorial to the "Queen of Sunday," an ordinary woman whose powerful singing is silenced by violence, while Gerald Barrax dedicates his more playful "Black Angels" to great blues and jazz singers.

The presentation of angels in African-American writing has also shared in the changing conventions, and fads, of American literary history. James Monroe Whitfield, a devoted abolitionist, writes firmly within the tradition of romantic idealism in "To My Beloved," painting her as a cross between a Greek goddess and a Christian angel. Charlotte Forten Grimke, a member of a prominent abolitionist family, exemplifies the school of domestic sentimentalism glorifying hearth and motherhood in "The Angel's Visit." Paul Laurence Dunbar's "Banjo Song" exhibits the late nineteenth-century belief that dialect writing accurately portrays the life of ordinary people. The rage for dialect first brought Dunbar to fame; later, he believed, it entrapped black writers in a demeaning stereotype after white dialect writers, like Mark Twain, had moved on.

Some of the authors included in *Ebony Angels* are major writers or historical figures; some have long been famous, and some have only recently been rediscovered. Little known poet George Moses Horton, for example, possesses what is possibly the most unusual of all American literary biographies: illiterate until his thirties, he supported himself by composing, in his head and on the spot, love lyrics and other poems for students at the University of North Carolina. Nonetheless, Horton was the first African American to publish a book of poetry in America. (Phillis Wheatley's earlier volume had been published in Great Britain.)

Angels also appear, however, in the powerful work of well-known Harlem Renaissance poets like Countee Cullen and Langston Hughes. They appear in a poem by 1960s radical Amiri Baraka (LeRoi Jones); they appear in the work of Robert Hayden, increasingly regarded as one of the most powerful American poets of his generation. And they appear in the work of contemporary women writers like Ntozake Shange and Toni Morrison, who seek to recover the roots of African spirituality and fuse it with elements of Christian imagery.

The selections in *Ebony Angels* have been chosen to reflect the major themes in African-American writing about angels during the last two hundred years. They have been chosen, in addition, to illustrate the wide variety of authors who have engaged these themes, and the forms in which they have done so. A few selections are highly individual; most, however, relate to either the important spiritual interests of African-American Christianity or to important developments in African-American history. In very different ways, each fulfills the most important criteria of the literature of angels: It expresses faith in God's care for humankind and provides insight into the spiritual dimension of human life.

Faith Jaycox

FOR HIS ANGELS ARE ALL
MINISTERING SPIRITS, SENT FORTH
TO MINISTER TO THEM THAT SHALL BE
HEIRS OF SALVATION.

——*George White, 1810*

ARRIVAL

Maya Angelou

Angels gather.
The rush of mad air
cyclones through.
Wing tips brush the
hair, a million
strands
stand; waving black anemones.
Hosannahs crush the
shell's ear tender, and
tremble
down clattering
to the floor.

Harps sound,
undulate their
sensuous meanings.
Hallelujah! Hallelujah!
You
beyond the door.

1983

from Saint Peter Relates an Incident of the Resurrection Day

James Weldon Johnson

The day came to a close.
And heaven—hell too—was filled with them that rose.
I shut the pearly gate and turned the key;
For Time was now merged into Eternity.

I gave one last look over the jasper wall,
And afar descried a figure dark and tall:
The unknown soldier, dust-stained and begrimed,
Climbing his way to heaven, and singing as he climbed:

> *Deep river, my home is over Jordan,*
> *Deep river, I want to cross over into camp-ground.*

Climbing and singing—

> *Deep river, my home is over Jordan,*
> *Deep river, I want to cross over into camp-ground. . . .*

I rushed to the gate and flung it wide,
Singing, he entered with a loose, long stride;
Singing and swinging up the golden street,
The music married to the tramping of his feet.

Tall, black soldier-angel marching alone,

Swinging up the golden street, saluting at the great white
  throne,

Singing, singing, singing, singing clear and strong.

Singing, singing, singing, till heaven took up the song:

> *Deep river, my home is over Jordan,*
>
> *Deep river, I want to cross over into camp-ground.*

1930

RELIGION MAKES MEN ANGELS

Ann Plato

Religion raises men above themselves: irreligion sinks them beneath the brutes. The one makes them angels; the other makes them evil spirits. *This* binds them down to a poor pitiable speck of perishable earth; *that* opens up a vista to the skies, and lets loose all the principles of an immortal mind, among the glorious objects of an eternal world.

*from "*RELIGION,*" 1841*

from SISTER LOU

Sterling Brown

Honey
Don't be feared of them pearly gates,
Don't go 'round to de back,
No mo'dataway
Not evah no mo'.

Let Michael tote yo' burden
An' yo' pocketbook an' evahthing
'Cept yo' Bible,
While Gabriel blows somp'n
Solemn but loudsome
On dat horn of his'n.

Honey
Go straight on to de Big House,
An' speak to yo' God
Widout no fear an' tremblin'.

Then sit down
An' pass de time of day awhile.

1932

*L*ORD, IS THIS HEAVEN?

A Spiritual

Lord, is this heaven
Oh Lord, is this heaven
Lord, is this heaven
Have I got here at last?

Sit down chile, sit down
Sit down chile, sit down
Sit down chile, sit down
Good Lord, I can't sit down.

Good Lord my long white robe
You know what you promise me.

Run angel and get a robe
And let her try it on.

Good Lord my angel wings
Oh, you know what you promise me.

Run angel and get them wings
And let her try them on.

TRADITIONAL

Dawn

Paul Laurence Dunbar

An angel, robed in spotless white,
Bent down and kissed the sleeping Night.
Night woke to blush; the sprite was gone.
Men saw the blush and called it Dawn.

1896

An Angel Teaches the Animals to Speak

Mary Weston Fordham

The earth was young, the world was fair,
And balmy breezes filled the air,
Nature reposed in solitude,
When God pronounced it "very good."

But silence reigned, nor beast nor bird
Had from its mate a whisper heard,
E'en man, God's image from above,
Could not, to Eve, tell of his love.

But lo! a light from 'mid the trees,
But hark! A rustling 'mongst the leaves,

Then a fair Angel from above,
Descending, sang his song of love.

Forth sprang the fierce beasts from their lair,
Bright feathered songsters fill the air,
All nature stirred to centre rang
When the celestial song began.

The Lion, monarch of the plain,
First tried to imitate the strain,
And shaking high his mane he roared,
Till beast and bird around him cowered.

The little Linnet tuned her lay,
The Lark, in turn, did welcome day,
And cooing soft, the timid Dove,
Did to his mate tell of his love.

The anthems from the earth so rare,
Higher and higher filled the air,
Till Seraphs caught the inspiring strain,
And morning stars together sang.

Only the fishes in the deep
Did not arouse them from their sleep,
So they alas! did never hear
Of the Angel's visit to this sphere.
Nor have they ever said one word
To mate or man, or beast or bird.

from "THE SAXON LEGEND OF LANGUAGE," 1897

from PRAISE OF CREATION

George Moses Horton

When each revolving wheel
    Assumed its sphere sublime,
Submissive Earth then heard the peal,
    And struck the march of time.

The march in heaven begun,
    And splendor filled the skies,
When Wisdom bade the morning Sun
    With joy from chaos rise.

The angels heard the tune
    Throughout creation ring:
They seized their golden harps as soon
    And touched on every string.

When time and space were young,
    And music rolled along—
The morning stars together sung,
    And Heaven was drown'd in song.

1829

from BANISHMENT OF MAN FROM THE GARDEN OF THE LORD

James Madison Bell

'Tis done! and yielding to their fate,
They move in silence toward the gate:
The Angel follows in command,
To watch and guard with sword in hand.

The exit gained, they're driven hence
Amid a darkness most intense;
No hand to guide, no angel voice
To urge them to the better choice;

But hand in hand, together they
Groped through the night their dubious way—
Huge spectral forms before them rise
Like hideous monsters to the skies,

While prowling beasts in quest of prey
Fill night with terror and dismay;
O! how dreadful must have been
That first night, in a world of sin.

1901

THE SINGER

Gerald Barrax

for Nina, Roberta, Aretha.
Sarah, Ella, Carmen.
Dinah, Billie, Bessie. And Ma.

Black Angel
Doing what she's gotta do
The sister sings

"Like a stone bird"
He said, intending to praise her.
But no bird has such a choice.

They speak, too,
Or whatever twittering means
But does that explain human song?

Maybe this more than natural impulse
Surprised even the creator
Who let the possibility

Slip his mind.
Not unintended.
Just not thought of.

. . . suppose Eve.
Giving a name
to something dull Adam
didn't know about:

What's that? What are you doing?

And she, holding the doomed child,
stopped and looked at him as if listening
and smiled, and said

Singing.

Not like birds
Who are doomed to sing
Her doom and ours is her silence.
      The sisters sing
      Doing what they've gotta do
      Black Angels

1980

REMEMBERING THE BIRTH
OF LUCIFER

Lucille Clifton

some will remember
the flash of light
as he broke
from the littlest finger
of God   some will
recall the bright shimmer
and then
flush in the tremble of air
so much shine

even then   the seraphim say
they knew
it was too much for
one small heaven
they rustled their three wings
they say   and began
to wait   and to watch

1991

from The Shroud of Color

Countee Cullen

I scarce dared trust my ears or eyes for awe
Of what they heard, and dread of what they saw;
For, privileged beyond degree, this flesh
Beheld God and His heaven in the mesh
Of Lucifer's revolt, saw Lucifer
Glow like the sun, and like a dulcimer
I heard his sin-sweet voice break on the yell
Of God's great warriors: Gabriel,
Saint Clair and Michael, Israfel and Raphael.
And strange it was to see God with His back
Against a wall, to see Christ hew and hack
Till Lucifer, pressed by the mighty pair,
And losing inch by inch, clawed at the air
With fevered wings; then, lost beyond repair,
He tricked a mass of stars into his hair;
He filled his hands with stars, crying as he fell,
"A star's a star although it burns in hell."

1925

The Devil and His Angels

W. E. B. Du Bois

I believe in the Devil and his angels, who wantonly work to narrow the opportunity of struggling human beings, especially if they be black; who spit in the faces of the fallen, strike them that cannot strike again, believe the worst and work to prove it, hating the image which their Maker stamped on a brother's soul.

from "CREDO," *1920*

Enslaving Angels

Henry Highland Garnet

Great God! I would as soon attempt to enslave GABRIEL or MICHAEL as to enslave a man made in the image of God, and for whom Christ died. Slavery is snatching man from the high place to which he was lifted by the hand of God, and dragging him down to the level of the brute creation.

from A MEMORIAL DISCOURSE DELIVERED IN THE HALL OF THE HOUSE OF REPRESENTATIVES, *February 12, 1865*

from *A* POEM ON THE FUGITIVE SLAVE LAW

Elymas Payson Rogers

Is that Bill law? Hark! from below
The voice of Lucifer cries, "No!
That Bill is a complete gewgaw,
Unworthy of the name of law,
And certainly I ought to know,
'Twas manufactured here below,
And then to leading statesmen sent
Who urged it 'to the full extent.'
Some think it binding to the letter;
But here in Tophet we know better,
For, we are better lawyers far,
Than half the Philadelphia bar:
The meanest devil can explain
Law more correctly than Judge Kane;
We like the Act, it suits us well;
For, 'tis a measure fresh from hell."

1855

God's Ministering Angels

Frederick Douglass

From my earliest recollection, I date the entertainment of a deep conviction that slavery would not always be able to hold me within its foul embrace; and in the darkest hours of my career in slavery, this living word of faith and spirit of hope departed not from me, but remained like ministering angels to cheer me through the gloom. This good spirit was from God, and to him I offer thanksgiving and praise.

from Narrative of the Life of
Frederick Douglass, 1845

Let God's Saints Come In

A Spiritual

Come down, Angel, and trouble the water,
Come down, Angel, and trouble the water,
(God say you must) Come down, Angel, and trouble the
  water,
And let God's saints come in.

Traditional

The Spirit of Harriet's Father Urges Her to Escape Slavery

Harriet Jacobs

The graveyard was in the woods, and twilight was coming on. Nothing broke the death-like stillness except the occasional twitter of a bird. My spirit was overawed by the solemnity of the scene. For more than ten years I had frequented this spot, but never had it seemed to me so sacred as now. A black stump, at the head of my mother's grave, was all that remained of a tree my father had planted. His grave was marked by a small wooden board, bearing his name, the letters of which were nearly obliterated. I knelt down and kissed them, and poured forth a prayer to God for guidance and support in the perilous step I was about to take. As I passed the wreck of the old meeting house, where, before Nat Turner's time, the slaves had been allowed to meet for worship, I seemed to hear my father's voice come from it, bidding me not to tarry till I reached freedom or the grave. I rushed on with renovated hopes. My trust in God had been strengthened by that prayer among the graves.

from INCIDENTS IN THE LIFE OF A SLAVE GIRL, *1861*

The Death of Moses

Frances E. W. Harper

He stood upon the highest peak of Nebo,
And saw the Jordan chafing through its gorges,
Its banks made bright by scarlet blooms
And purple blossoms. . . .
Gazed he on the lovely landscape
Till it faded from his view, and the wing
Of death's sweet angel hovered o'er the mountain's
Crest, and he heard his garments rustle through
The watches of the night.

                  Then another, fairer, vision
Broke upon his longing gaze; 'twas the land
Of crystal fountains, love and beauty, joy
And light, for the pearly gates flew open,
And his ransomed soul went in. And when the morning
O'er the mountain fringed each crag and peak with light,
Cold and lifeless lay the leader. God had touched
His eyes with slumber, giving his beloved sleep.

      Oh never on that mountain
      Was seen a lovelier sight
      Than the troupe of fair young angels
      That gathered 'round the dead.
      With gentle hands they bore him

That bright and shining train,
From Nebo's lonely mountain
To sleep in Moab's vale.
But they sang no mournful dirges,
No solemn requiems said.
And the soft waves of their pinions
Made music as they trod.
But no one heard them passing,
None saw their chosen grave;
It was the angels secret
Where Moses should be laid.
And when the grave was finished,
They trod with golden sandals
Above the sacred spot,
And the brightest, fairest flower
Sprang up beneath their tread.
Nor broken turf, nor hillock
Did e'er reveal that grave,
And truthful lips have never said
We know where he is laid.

from MOSES: A STORY OF THE NILE, *1869*

from THE ANGEL'S MESSAGE

Clara Ann Thompson

There's a wonderful story,
  That never grows old,
Though centuries have passed,
  Since first it was told;
Since the angel of God,
  On that far, early morn,
Proclaimed to the shepherds,
  That Jesus was born.
Ah, the news was too great
  For poor mortal to bring!
An angel must tell
  Of the birth of the King.

1908

Angels Announce the Birth of Christ

Alfred Gibbs Campbell

From Heaven's high mansions to the earth below
An angel band, on gladsome errand bound,
Sped to the plains where, seated on the ground,
The humble shepherds through the solemn night
Watched their loved flocks, and gathered pure delight
And holy wisdom, which each glowing star
Rained on them with its radiance from afar.
Around the shepherds shone celestial light,
(Each gem eclipsing in the crown of night),
Making them quake with apprehensive dread,
But momentary, for God's angel said,
"Fear not, I bring glad tiding unto all
People who dwell on this terrestrial ball."
Then Heaven's high dome with sounds harmonic rang
As the angelic host in concert sang
"Glory to God! Good-will and peace on earth!"
Most fitting song to usher in the birth
Of heaven's divinest Son, whose mission grand
Eternal Love had from eternal planned!

from "The Divine Mission," *1852*

from *An* Evening Thought

Jupiter Hammon

Salvation comes by Christ alone,
The only Son of God;
Redemption now to every one,
That love his holy Word.

Ten Thousand Angels cry to Thee,
Yea louder than the Ocean.
Thou are the Lord, we plainly see;
Thou are the true Salvation.

Come Blessed Jesus, Heavenly Dove,
Accept Repentance here;
Salvation give, with tender Love;
Let us with Angels share. Finis.

1761

ON BEING BROUGHT FROM AFRICA TO AMERICA

Phillis Wheatley

'Twas mercy brought me from my *Pagan* land,
Taught my benighted soul to understand
That there's a God, that there's a *Saviour* too:
Once I redemption neither sought nor knew.
Some view our sable race with scornful eye,
"Their colour is a diabolic die."
Remember, *Christians, Negros,* black as *Cain,*
May be refin'd, and join th' angelic train.

1773

FOR A LADY I KNOW

Countee Cullen

She even thinks that up in heaven
  Her class lies late and snores,
While poor black cherubs rise at seven
  To do celestial chores.

1925

An Angel Brings a Call to Preach the Gospel

Julia Foote

When called of God, on a particular occasion, to a definite work, I said, "No, Lord, not me." . . . I thought it could not be that I was called to preach—I, so weak and ignorant. Still, I knew all things were possible with God, even to confounding the wise by the foolish things of this earth. Yet in me there was a shrinking.

I took all my doubts and fears to the Lord in prayer, when, what seemed to be an angel, made his appearance. In his hand was a scroll, on which were these words: "Thee have I chosen to preach my Gospel without delay." The moment my eyes saw it, it appeared to be printed on my heart. The angel was gone in an instant, and I, in agony, cried out, "Lord, I cannot do it!"

From that day my appetite failed me and sleep fled from my eyes. I seemed as one tormented. . . .

One night, as I lay weeping and beseeching the dear Lord to remove this burden from me, there appeared the same angel that came to me before, and on his breast were these words: "You are lost unless you obey God's righteous commands." . . .

I had always been opposed to the preaching of women, . . . This rose before me like a mountain, and when I thought of the

difficulties they had to encounter, both from professors and non-professors, I shrank back and cried, "Lord, I cannot go!"

He . . . sent the angel again with this message: "You have I chosen to go in my name and warn the people of their sins." I bowed my head and said, "I will go, Lord."

That moment I felt a joy and peace I had not known for months.

from A Brand Plucked from the Fire,
An Autobiographical Sketch, *1886*

Balaam, the Angel, and Female Preachers

Jarena Lee

I have heard that as far back as Adam Clarke's time, his objections to female preaching were met by the answer—"If an ass reproved Balaam, and a barn-door fowl reproved Peter, why should not a woman reprove sin?" I do not introduce this for its complementary classification of women with donkeys and fowls, but to give the reply of a poor woman, who had once been a slave. To the first companion she said—"May be a speaking woman is like an ass—but I can tell you one thing, the ass seen the angel when Balaam didn't."

from Religious Experience and Journal
of Mrs. Jarena Lee, Giving an Account of
Her Call to Preach the Gospel, *1849*

CONFESSION

Lucille Clifton

father
i am not equal to the faith required.
i doubt.
i have a woman's certainties;
bodies pulled from me,
pushed into me.
bone flesh is what i know.

father
the angels say they have no wings.
i woke one morning
feeling how to see them.
i could discern their shadows
in the shadow. i am not
equal to the faith required.

father
i see your mother standing now
shoulderless and shoeless by your side.
i hear her whisper truths i cannot know.
father i doubt.

father
what are the actual certainties?
your mother speaks of love.

the angels say they have no wings.
i am not equal to the faith required.
i try to run from such surprising presence;
the angels stream before me
like a torch.

1987

ON THE ROAD TO DAMASCUS

Rita Dove

*And it came to pass, that, as I made my journey, and
was come nigh unto Damascus about noon, suddenly
there shone from heaven a great light round about me.
And I fell to the ground . . .*
— ACTS 22:6–7

They say I was struck down by the voice of an angel:
      flames poured through the radiant fabric of heaven
As I cried out and fell to my knees.

My first recollection was of Unbroken Blue—
      but two of the guards have already sworn by
the tip of my tongue set ablaze. . . .

I was a Roman and had my business

among the clouded towers of Damascus.
      I had not counted on earth rearing,
honey streaming down a parched sky,

a spear skewering me to the dust of the road
      on the way to the city I would never
enter now, her markets steaming with vendors

and compatriots in careless armor lifting a hand
     in greeting as they call out my name,
only to find no one home.

1989

ANGEL DONE CHANGE MY NAME

A Spiritual

Angel done change my name
Angel done change my name
Done change my name from natural to grace,
Angel done change my name.

TRADITIONAL

An Angel Teaches a Slave to Read the Bible

John Jea

the Lord was pleased in his infinite mercy, to send an angel, in a vision, in shining raiment, and his countenance shining as the sun, with a large bible in his hands, and brought it unto me, and said, *"I am come to bless thee, and to grant thee thy request,"* as you read in the Scriptures. . . . although the place was dark as a dungeon, I awoke, as the Scripture saith, and found it illuminated with the light of the glory of God, and the angel standing by me, with the large book open, which was the Holy Bible, and said unto me, *"Thou hast desired to read and understand this book, and to speak the language of it both in English and in Dutch; I will therefore teach thee, and now read;"* and then he taught me to read the first chapter of the gospel according to St. John; and when I had read the whole chapter, the angel and book were both gone in the twinkling of an eye. . . .

from The Life, History, and Unparalleled Sufferings of John Jea, the African Preacher, *1815*

*L*AZARUS VISITS HELL
WITH ISRAFEL,
THE ANGEL OF MUSIC

Fenton Johnson

Quick from a crater red with belching fire
A hornèd form bestrided upper Hell;
His eye was dark and pierced me like a bolt
Of lightning in an angry summer storm;
Like thunder in the cave of Sinai
He roared and all the depths of Sheol shook.

The angel trembled not, but stood his ground. . . .
A better weapon had this singing soul
The mystery and sweetness of his voice,
Which loosened charms the roaring elements,
He sang a song so weird and strange and grand,
The devil cowered, wond'ring at the spell . . .
And Satan blinded by the angel spell
Seized me, and tore to shreds my holiness.
Poor Israfel when this he saw wept loud
But God above had turned His willing ear;
I heard the Master's voice like thunder roll,
Into my dreaming, "Lazarus, come forth."

from "The Vision of Lazarus," 1913

from NIGHT

Josephine D. Heard

The shades of eve are quickly closing in,
    And streaks of silver gild the eastern sky,
Belated songsters have their vespers sung
    With happy hearts and silvery noted tongue,
The busy world has ceased its toil and din,
    And guardian angels now their watch begin.

1890

from THE ANGEL'S VISIT

Charlotte L. Forten Grimke

"On such a night as this," methought,
    "Angelic forms are near;
In beauty unrevealed to us
    They hover in the air.
O mother, loved and lost," I cried,
    "Methinks thou'rt near me now;
Methinks I feel thy cooling touch
    Upon my burning brow."

I ceased: then o'er my sense stole
  A soothing dreamy spell,
And gently to my ear were borne
  The tones I loved so well;
A sudden flood of rosy light
  Filled all the dusky wood,
And, clad in shining robes of white,
  My angel mother stood.

She gently drew me to her side,
  She pressed her lips to mine,
And softly said, "Grieve not, my child;
  A mother's love is thine.

"For thee a brighter day's in store;
  And every earnest soul
That presses on, with purpose high,
  Shall gain the wished-for goal.
And thou, beloved, faint not beneath
  The weary weight of care;
Daily before our Father's throne
  I breathe for thee a prayer."

She paused, and fondly bent on me
  One lingering look of love,
Then softly said,—and passed away,—
  "Farewell! we'll meet above." . . .

1858

My Angel

Jonathan Henderson Brooks

That night my angel stooped and strained
To lift me from the mud.
He could not lift my heaviness.
My angel sweated blood.
He said: You are the heaviest grief
In heaven since the flood.

All night my angel stooped and strained,
Loath to abandon me:
The heaviest load since Lucifer
Shook heaven's regency.
All night he interceded for
My black necessity.

He rose. And two wings hid his feet.
And two wings veiled his face,
And two wings took him, weary wings,
To angels' resting place.
He flew away. He left with me
Despair and my disgrace.

1948

from Mourning Poem for the Queen of Sunday

Robert Hayden

Lord's lost Him His mockingbird,
His fancy warbler;
Satan sweet-talked her,
four bullets hushed her.
Who would have thought
she'd end that way?

Four bullets hushed her. And the world a-clang with evil.
Who's going to make old hardened sinner men tremble now
and the righteous rock?
Oh who and oh who will sing Jesus down
to help with struggling and doing without and being colored
all through blue Monday?
Till way next Sunday?

All those angels
in their cretonne clouds and finery
the true believer saw
when she rared back her head and sang,
all those angels are surely weeping.
Who would have thought
she'd end that way? . . .

1962

A LOAD OF ANGELS AND THE WORD "UNH HUNH"

Zora Neale Hurston

Ole Devil looked around Hell one day and seen his place was short of help so he thought he'd run up to Heben and kidnap some angels to keep things runnin' tell he got reinforcements from Miami.

Well, he slipped up on a great crowd of angels on de outskirts of Heben and stuffed a couple of thousand in his mouth, a few hundred under each arm and wrapped his tail 'round another thousand and darted off towards Hell.

When he was flyin' low over de earth lookin' for a place to land, a man looked up and seen de Devil and ast 'im, "Ole Devil, Ah see you got a load of angels. Is you goin' back for mo'?"

Devil opened his mouth and tole 'im, "Yeah," and all de li'l angels flew out his mouf and went on back to Heben. While he was tryin' to ketch 'em he lost all de others. So he went back after another load.

He was flyin' low agin and de same man seen him and says, "Ole Devil, Ah see you got another load uh angels."

Devil nodded his head and said "unh hunh," and dat's why we say it today.

from MULES AND MEN, *1935*

*B*LOW YOUR TRUMPET, GABRIEL

A Spiritual of the First South Carolina Volunteer Regiment

O Satan is a liar, and he conjure too,
And if you don't mind, he'll conjure you.
So blow your trumpet, Gabriel,
  Blow your trumpet louder;
And I want that trumpet to blow me home
  To my new Jerusalem.

O, I was lost in the wilderness,
King Jesus hand me the candle down.
O, blow your trumpet, Gabriel,
  Blow your trumpet louder;
And I want that trumpet to blow me home
  To my new Jerusalem.

from T. W. HIGGINSON, ARMY LIFE
IN A BLACK REGIMENT, *1869*

ANGELS WINGS

Langston Hughes

The angels wings is white as snow,
    O, white as snow,
       White
         as
             snow.

The angels wings is white as snow,
    But I drug ma wings
    In the dirty mire.
    O, I drug ma wings
    All through the fire.
But the angels wings is white as snow,
    White
       as
         snow.

1927, 1959

from RECKLESS BLUES

Bessie Smith

My mama says I'm reckless
My daddy says I'm wild.
I ain't good lookin' but I'm
Somebody's angel child.

RECORDED *1925*

To My Beloved

James Monroe Whitfield

A vision as of angel bright
    Sudden appears before my face,
A beauteous, fascinating sprite,
    Endowed with every charm and grace.

And when those matchless charms I viewed,
    Thy faultless form, and graceful mien,
Surprised, amazed, entranced I stood,
    And gazed with rapture on the scene.

And when they lips were ope'd to speak,
    In tones so sweet, so soft and clear,
Gabriel his golden harp might break,
    And seraphs lean from heaven to hear.

'Tis the pure mind which dwells within,
    Displays itself in act and word,
And raises thee from every sin
    Far, *far* above the common herd.

1853

from *A* BANJO SONG

Paul Laurence Dunbar

When de quiet, restful shadders
      Is beginnin' jes' to fall—
Den I take de little banjo
      From its place upon de wall.

Den my family gadders roun' me
      In de fadin' o' de light,
As I strike de strings to try 'em
      If dey all is tuned er-right.
An' it seems we're so nigh heaven
      We kin hear de angels sing
When de music o' dat banjo
      Sets my cabin all er-ring.

Now, de blessed little angels
      Up in heaven, we are told,
Don't do nothin' all dere lifetime
      'Ceptin' play on harps o' gold.
Now I think heaven'd be mo' homelife
      If we'd hear some music fall
From a real ol'-fashioned banjo,
      Like dat one upon de wall.

1895

House What's Built Without Hands

A Spiritual

I want that house what's built without hands
    Oh, built by the hammer of the angels
    Oh, built by the hammer of the angels
    Oh, built by the hammer of the angels.

TRADITIONAL

from Thank God for Little Children

Frances E. W. Harper

Thank God for little children;
    Bright flowers by earth's wayside,
The dancing, joyous lifeboats
    Upon life's stormy tide.

I almost think the angels,
    Who tend life's garden fair,
Drop down the sweet wild blossoms
    That bloom around us here.

1871

WHERE DO SCHOOL DAYS END?

Josephine D. Heard

A little child sat on the floor,
Turning the pages o'er and o'er,
Of Mother Goose's nursery book;
He raised his eyes with puzzled look,
And said, "Mamma, attention lend,
And tell me: Where do school days end?"

"My boy, that is no easy task—
A weighty question 'tis you ask;
For every day adds to our store
Of knowledge gained the day before;
So you must ask some wiser friend
To tell you, where school days will end."

The parson came that very day,
His usual pastoral call to pay;
The child stole in with cunning look.
And on a stool his seat he took,
"Sir, will you information lend,
And tell me, where school days will end?"

"There is a land of light you know,
Where all good people are to go—

Where little children rob'd in white,
Are ever happy in God's sight.
And when you die He'll angels send
To take you where school days shall end."

1890

On the
Sanctified Knowledge of
Ministers

Bishop Daniel A. Payne

Lord Bacon, one of England's greatest philosophers, has said that "Knowledge is power." . . .

Permit me humbly to add, that sanctified knowledge is a power at once beneficent, glorious, and tremendous. It is beneficent, because it is always delighting in good works, and conferring blessings upon mankind—it is glorious, because it shines forth with the brightness of the unclouded sun;—it is tremendous, because the man in whom it dwells is like an angel of God, armed with thunderbolts, crushing the strong-holds of the empire of Satan.

from The First Annual Address to the
Philadelphia Annual Conference of the
AME Church, *May 16, 1853*

THE POET VIEWS HIS MOTHER'S
YEARBOOK PHOTO

from **LEROY**

Amiri Baraka

I wanted to know my mother when she sat
looking sad across the campus in the late 20's
into the future of the soul, there were black angels
straining above her head, carrying life from our ancestors,
and knowledge. . . .

                        Hypnotizing me, from so far
ago, from that vantage of knowledge passed on to her passed
   on
to me and all the other black people of our time.

1969

ℱIT WORK FOR MEN
AND ANGELS

The Committee of the Colored National Convention,
Frederick Douglass and Others

It is more than a mere figure of speech to say, that we are as a people, chained together. . . . As one rises, all must rise, and as one falls all must fall. . . . Every one of us should be ashamed to consider himself free, while his brother is a slave. The wrongs of our brethren should be our constant theme. There should be no time too precious, no calling too holy, no place too sacred, to make room for this cause. We should not only feel it to be the cause of humanity, but the cause of christianity, and fit work for men and angels.

from AN ADDRESS TO THE COLORED PEOPLE
OF THE UNITED STATES, *September 6, 1848*

from A PRAYER FOR THE SLAVE

Joseph Cephas Holly

Angels of the celestial band,
    Come visit earth in trains,
And loose the fetters of the hand!
    Which bears oppression's chains.
Proclaim that all men shall be free,—
    Nor freedom's blessings lack,
No matter of what clime they be,
    Nor whether white or black,
Waft the glad tidings o'er the land,
    Through the loud trumpet's mouth;
Liberty to the fettered band,
From north to farthest south.

1853

IN COMMEMORATION OF THE ABOLITION
OF SLAVERY IN THE BRITISH WEST
INDIA ISLES

from THE DAWN OF FREEDOM

James Madison Bell

Then Freedom's joyous angel flew
    With lightning speed o'er land and wave,

And loud her clarion trumpet blew,
  And woke to life each panting slave.
Woke them to life? They did not sleep,
  But there in anxious silence stood,
Waiting the welcome sound to sweep
  Athwart Atlantic's briny flood.

And when the sound fell on their ear,
They laughed, they wept, they knelt in prayer;
And rising from their bended knees,
They sang in joyous ecstacies,
'Till hill and vale and distant plain
Gave back the gladsome sound again.

For shining ones of heavenly birth
  Bent o'er the jasper walls on high,
And caught the jubilant songs of earth,
  And bore them upward to the sky;

And Heaven gave audience to the strain
  Of those fair minstrels as they sang,
Gathering up the glad refrain
  With which the hills and valleys rang,
And sending them forever on,
  And on, and on, eternally;
For Heaven itself can boast no song
  Of sweeter strain than Liberty.

1868

BROTHER FREEDOM
(FOR MALCOLM)

Margaret T. Burroughs

Lay him down gently, lay him down slow.
Swathe him in linen, wrap him just so.
Turn his young face toward Mecca's soft glow.
Our fallen warrior, our Brother Freedom. . . .

I for one did not agree
With all the things he said,
But I defend his right to speak out
Without paying the price he paid. Brother Freedom. . . .

Immortal now, he sits in fine company
With L'Ouverture and Joseph Cinque
With Vesey, Turner, and Prosser
Lumumba and Evers and others. Brother Freedom.

Brother Freedom is dead. Brother Freedom lives.
His is a spirit that swirls around us
In the vital air, inspiring all
Who seek, salute Freedom. Brother Freedom.

1969

from Eulogy for the Martyred Children

Reverend Dr. Martin Luther King, Jr.

Your children did not live long, but they lived well. The quantity of their lives was disturbingly small, but the quality of their lives was magnificently big. Where they died and what they were doing when death came will remain a marvelous tribute to each of you and an eternal epitaph to each of them. They died not in a den or dive nor were they hearing and telling filthy jokes at the time of their death. They died within the sacred walls of the church after discussing a principle as eternal as love.

Shakespeare had Horatio utter some beautiful words over the dead body of Hamlet. I paraphrase these words today as I stand over the last remains of these lovely girls.

"Good-night sweet princesses; may the flight of angels take thee to thy eternal rest."

from A Sermon Delivered at the Funeral of the Four Children Killed in the Bombing of a Baptist Church in Birmingham, Alabama, *September 1963*

Send One Angel Down

A Spiritual

Oh-o Lord Send one angel down
Oh-o Lord Send one angel down
Oh-o Lord Send one angel down
Send him in a hurry,
Send him in a hurry.

Oh-o Lord this is the needed time
Send him in a hurry.

Oh-o Lord I'm in trouble now
Send him in a hurry.

Oh-o Lord I need lil' more faith
Send him in a hurry.

Oh-o Lord Send one angel down
Oh-o Lord Send one angel down
Oh-o Lord Send one angel down
Send him in a hurry,
Send him in a hurry.

TRADITIONAL

RELIGION, THE DAUGHTER OF HEAVEN

Ann Plato

Religion is the daughter of Heaven—parent of our virtues, and source of all true felicity. She alone giveth peace and contentment; divests the heart of anxious cares, bursts on the mind a flood of joy, and sheds unmingled and preternatural sunshine in the pious breast. By her the spirits of darkness are banished from the earth, and angelic ministers of grace thicken, unseen, the regions of mortality.

from "RELIGION," *1841*

The Death of Jesus: A Sermon

Zora Neale Hurston

I can see Him as He mounted Calvary and hung upon de
    cross for our sins.
I can see-eee-ee
De mountains fall to their rocky knees when He cried
"My God, my God! Why hast Thou forsaken me?"
The mountains fell to their rocky knees and trembled like
    a beast
From the stroke of the master's axe
One angel took the flinches of God's eternal power
And bled the veins of the earth
One angel that stood at the gate with a flaming sword
Was so well pleased with his power
Until he pierced the moon with his sword
And she ran down in blood
And de sun
Batted her fiery eyes and put on her judgment robe
And laid down in de cradle of eternity
And rocked herself into sleep and slumber
He died until the great belt in the wheel of time
And de geological strata fell aloose
And a thousand angels rushed to de canopy of heben

With flamin' swords in their hands
And placed their feet upon blue ether's bosom,
    and looked back at de dazzlin' throne
And de arc angels had veiled their faces
And de throne was draped in mournin'
And de orchestra had struck silence for the space of
    half an hour
Angels had lifted their harps to de weepin' willows
And God had looked off to-wards immensity
And blazin' worlds fell off His teeth
And about that time Jesus groaned on de cross, and
Dropped His head in the locks of His shoulder and said,
    "It is finished, it is finished."

from JONAH'S GOURD VINE, *1934*

from THE RESURRECTION

Jonathan Henderson Brooks

A muffled whiff of sudden breath
Ruffled the passive air of death.

He woke, and raised Himself in bed;
      Recalled how He was crucified;
Touched both hands' fingers to His head,
      And lightly felt his fresh-healed side.

Then with a deep, triumphant sigh,
He coolly put His grave-clothes by—
Folded the sweet, white winding sheet,
      The toweling, the linen bands,
      The napkin, all with careful hands—
And left the borrowed chamber neat.

His steps were like the breaking day:
      So soft across the watch He stole,
      He did not wake a single soul,
Nor spill one dewdrop by the way.

Now Calvary was loveliness:
      Lilies that flowered thereupon
Pulled off the white moon's pallid dress,
      And put the morning's vesture on.

"Why seek the living among the dead?
He is not here," the angel said.

The early winds took up the words,
And bore them to the lilting birds,
The leafing trees, and everything
That breathed the living breath of spring.

1948

ℐHE ANGEL ROLL THE
STONE AWAY

A Spiritual

The angel roll the stone away,
The angel roll the stone away,
'Twas on a bright an' shiny morn,
When the trumpet begin to sound,
The angel roll the stone away.

TRADITIONAL

GOD'S ANGEL VISITS DURING PRAYER

Noah Calwell Cannon

Some tell us that praying, and also that praising,
Is labor that's all spent in vain:
But we have such witness, that God hears with sweetness;
From praying we will not refrain.
There was old father Noah and ten thousand more,
Who witness'd that God heard them pray;
There was Samuel and Hannah, Paul, Silas and Peter,
And Daniel and Jonah, will say,
That God by his Spirit, and angel did visit
Their souls while in this happy frame.
Shall we all go a fainting, while they went a praising,
And glorified God in a flame!

from "THE ARK," *1833*

from WHEN OL' SIS' JUDY PRAY

James Edwin Campbell

When ol' Sis' Judy pray,
De thunders of Mount Sin-a-i
Comes rushin' down from up on high—
De Devil turn his back an' fly
While sinners loud for pardon cry
When ol' Sis' Judy pray.

When ol' Sis' Judy pray,
Salvation's light comes pourin' down—
Hit fill de church an' all de town—
Why, angels' robes go rustlin' 'roun',
An' heaven on de Earth am foun',
When ol' Sis' Judy pray.

When ol' Sis' Judy pray,
My soul go sweepin' up on wings,
An' loud de church wid "Glory!" rings,
An' wide de gates of Jahsper swings
Till you hear harps wid golden strings,
When ol' Sis' Judy pray.

1895

from T HE JUDGMENT DAY

James Weldon Johnson

Early one of these mornings,
God's a-going to call for Gabriel,
That tall, bright angel, Gabriel;
And God's a-going to say to him: Gabriel,
Blow your silver trumpet,
And wake the living nations.

And Gabriel's going to ask him: Lord,
How loud must I blow it?
And God's a-going to tell him: Gabriel,
Blow it calm and easy.
Then putting one foot on the mountain top,
And the other in the middle of the sea,
Gabriel's going to stand and blow his
horn,
To wake the living nations.

Then God's a-going to say to him: Gabriel,
Once more blow your silver trumpet,
And wake the nations underground.

And Gabriel's going to ask him: Lord
How loud must I blow it?

And God's a-going to tell him: Gabriel,
Like seven peals of thunder.
Then the tall, bright angel, Gabriel,
Will put one foot on the battlements of heaven
And the other on the steps of hell,
And blow that silver trumpet
Till he shakes old hell's foundations.

And I feel Old Earth a-shuddering—
And I see the graves a-bursting—
And I hear a sound,
A blood-chilling sound.
What is that sound I hear?
It's the clicking together of the dry bones,
Bone to bone—the dry bones.
And I see coming out of the bursting graves,
And marching up from the valley of death,
The army of the dead.
And the living and the dead in the twinkling of an eye
Are caught up in the middle of the air,
Before God's judgment bar.

Oh-o-oh, sinner,
Where will you stand,
In that great day when God's a-going to rain down fire?

1927

CHRIST DESCENDS ON JUDGMENT DAY

Maria Stewart

The day is coming, my friends, and I rejoice in that day, when the secrets of all hearts shall be manifested before saints and angels, men and devils. It will be a great day of joy and rejoicing to the humble followers of Christ, but a day of terror and dismay to hypocrites and unbelievers. Of that day and hour knoweth no man, no, not even the angels in heaven, but the Father only. . . .

Christ shall descend in the clouds of heaven, surrounded by ten thousand of his saints and angels, and it shall be very tempestuous round about him; and before him shall be gathered all nations, and kindred, and tongues, and people; and every knee shall bow, and every tongue confess. . . . The poor despised followers of Christ will not then regret their sufferings here; they shall be carried by angels into Abraham's bosom, and shall be comforted; and the Lord God shall wipe away their tears.

from AN ADDRESS DELIVERED BEFORE THE AFRIC-AMERICAN FEMALE INTELLIGENCE SOCIETY OF BOSTON, *September 21, 1832*

THE SHIP OF ZION

A Spiritual

It's the good ole ship of Zion,
It's the good ole ship of Zion,
It's the good ole ship of Zion,
     And she's makin' for the Promised Land.

She has angels for the sailors,
She has angels for the sailors,
She has angels for the sailors,
     And she's makin' for the Promised Land.

O King Jesus is the captain,
O King Jesus is the captain,
O King Jesus is the captain,
     And she's makin' for the Promised Land.

TRADITIONAL

Swing Low, Sweet Chariot

A Spiritual

Swing low, sweet chariot,
Comin' for to carry me home,
Swing low, sweet chariot,
Comin' for to carry me home.

I looked over Jordan, and what did I see,
Comin' for to carry me home,
A band of angels comin' after me,
Comin' for to carry me home.

TRADITIONAL

Ancestral Messengers/ Composition II

Ntozake Shange

they told me to travel toward the sun
to lift my feet from the soil
engage myself to the wind in a dance
called my own/
my legs, wings of lavender & mauve

they carried me to the sun-cave
the light sweet shadows eclipsing our tongues

we spoke of longings/yearning/the unknown
we spoke in the tongue of the snake
the hoot of the owl
tongues of our ancestors
dancing with the wind

we traverse the sun
fully fired violet beings
directly overhead the sun-cave
lifting me/coaxing my eyes
to see as theirs do

crisp stalking spirits/proud
swirling spirits/my blood

they've made themselves a home here
blood relatives converging
wherever my soul is lurking
telling me   now   yes   now
go to the center of the sun

we are sending sepia stallions
headstrong appaloosas and cypress carriages
to carry you home

1987

A FLAMING-FACED ANGEL

He's gone to the kingdom above,
In the raiment of angels,

(Voice of Sister)　　　　　In the raiment!
　　　　　In the raiment of angels!

To the region above,
An' he sleeps,—

(Voices chanting throughout congregation)
　　　　　Oh, he sleeps,—
　　　　　Oh, he sleeps!
　　　　　On the banks of a river!

Way de tall pines grow,
On the banks of a river.

(Congregation)　　　　　With the starry crowned angels,
　　　　　On the banks of a river.

An' the flowers is bloomin'
In the blood of the Lamb.

(Shrill voice of Sister and taken up by congregation
chanting and swaying)

                    The blood of the Lamb!
                    In the blood of the Lamb!

An' the birds is singin'
Wey de wind blows soft,
As the breath of an angel,
An' he sleeps!
Wey de tall pines grow,
On the banks of a river.

(Voice)   An' he sleeps!

(Another voice)   Wey de tall pines grow.

An' his sperrit is guarded,

(Several voices)   On the banks of a river.

By a flaming-faced angel.

(Sister)   Yes, Jesus, of a flaming-faced angel
                   On the banks of a river.

Standing on mountains of rest.

Transcribed *1927*

WHEN ALL GOD'S CHILLUN HAD WINGS

Toni Morrison

"Why did you call Solomon a flying African?"

"Oh, that's just some old folks' lie they tell around here. Some of those Africans they brought over here as slaves could fly. A lot of them flew back to Africa. The one around here who did was this same Solomon. . . ."

"When you say 'flew off' you mean he ran away, don't you? Escaped?"

"No, I mean flew. Oh, it's just foolishness, you know, but according to the story he wasn't running away. He was flying. He flew. You know, like a bird. Just stood up in the fields one day, ran up some hill, spun around a couple of times, and was lifted up in the air. Went right on back to wherever it was he came from."

from SONG OF SOLOMON, *1977*

ALL GOD'S CHILLUN GOT WINGS

A Spiritual

I got a robe, you got a robe
All of God's Chillun got a robe.
When I get to Heaven goin' to put on my robe,
I'm goin' to shout all over God's Heaven.

I got a harp, you got a harp
All of God's Chillun got a harp.
When I get to Heaven goin' to take up my harp,
I'm goin' to play all over God's Heaven.

I got-a wings, you got-a wings,
All of God's Chillun got-a wings.
When I get to Heaven goin' to put on my wings,
I'm goin' to fly all over God's Heaven.

Heaven, Heaven,
Everybody talkin' bout Heaven ain't goin' there;
Heaven, Heaven,
I'm goin' to fly all over God's Heaven.

TRADITIONAL

SPORTING BEASLEY

Sterling Brown

Good glory, give a look at Sporting Beasley
Strutting, oh my Lord.

> Tophat cocked one side his bulldog head,
> Striped four-in-hand, and in his buttonhole
> A red carnation; Prince Albert coat
> Form-fitting, corset like; vest snugly filled,
> Gray morning trousers, spotless and full-flowing.
> White spats and a cane.

Step it, Mr. Beasley, oh step it till the sun goes down. . . .

> Oh Jesus, when this brother's bill falls due,
> When he steps off the chariot
> And flicks the dust from his patent leathers with his
>   silk handkerchief,
> When he stands in front of the jasper gates, patting
>   his tie,
>
> And then paces in
> Cane and knees working like well-oiled slow-timed
>   pistons;

Lord help us, give a *look* at him.

> Don't make him dress up in no night gown, Lord.

Don't put no fuss and feathers on his shoulders,
Lord.

Let him know it's heaven.

Let him keep his hat, his vest, his elkstooth, and
everything.

Let him have his spats and cane
Let him have his spats and cane.

1932

Angels' Wings and Men's Shirts

A Folktale

There was the old black parson who used to describe both heaven and hell in great detail, as a "four-square city with the streets all gold, an' jasper walls, an' pearly gates, an' spires, an' temples, an' angels." His descriptions were so vivid that some of the sisters, going into various ecstacies and spasms and contortions, declared that they could fairly hear the flapping of the angels' wings.

And after the sermon was over and the collection was being taken, a devilish young fellow who had been seated in the rear of the church, came forward. . . . to ask the pastor a question. And so, stepping back a pace, he knitted his brow into a pretense of sincere puzzlement and said:

"Mr. Pastor, I sho' enjoyed your sermon this mornin', 'bout all them angels with all them wings. But there's one thing in your sermon what puzzles me, an' I wants to ask you 'bout it. What puzzles me, an' what I wants to know, is: When I gets to heaven, how in the world is I ever gwine to get my shirt on over all them wings?"

But the old parson not only had a gift for humor but he was also a good sport. He therefore looked over his spectacles at the boy, and replied:

"Look hyeah, boy, don't you be askin' no such fool questions as that in this church,—'cause in the first place, when you dies, that ain't a-gwine to be your problem nohow. When you dies, your problem's gwine to be: How in the world is you ever gwine to get your hat on over your horns! That's what's gwine to be your problem."

Collected *1926*

Lif' Up de Spade

Fenton Johnson

Lif' up de spade; throw down de dirt,
De Mastah's called me home at las'.
Lif' up de spade; throw down de dirt,
An' lay mah body 'neath de grass.
De angel's sittin' at mah foot,
Another's sittin' at mah head,
An' some one's croonin' mournful songs
Above de moun' dey call mah bed.

1916

The Fundamentalist

May Miller

When I pound on that great door,
Little white angels,
Let me come in.
Scrub my lying tongue
With brimstone and ashes,
Just let me in there.
Dunk me, One God

Of the Lamb and the Word,
Dunk me deep
In the living waters,
Then stand me tall
On the threshold of Heaven
Dripping the lies I done told.
Please, Sir, let me in.
Wipe my feet,
Bright angels of mercy;

Call me clean
Give me a new name,
Sweet risen Jesus,
So as I can come in.

     Amen.

1959

ANGELS WITNESS A SANCTIFICATION

Jarena Lee

But when this voice whispered in my heart, saying, "Pray for sanctification," I again bowed . . . and said "Lord *sanctify* my soul for Christ's sake." That very instant, as if lightning had darted through me, I sprang to my feet, and cried, "The Lord has sanctified my soul!" There was none to hear this but the angels who stood around to witness my joy—and Satan, whose malice raged the more. That Satan was there, I knew; for no sooner had I cried out "The Lord has sanctified my soul," than there seemed another voice behind me, saying, "No, it is too great a work to be done." But another spirit said "Bow down for the witness—I received it—*thou art sanctified!*"

from RELIGIOUS EXPERIENCE AND JOURNAL OF MRS. JARENA LEE, GIVING AN ACCOUNT OF HER CALL TO PREACH THE GOSPEL, *1849*

Singing Hallelujia

Fenton Johnson

I went down to Jordan,
    Singing, "Hallelujia!",
I went down to Jordan
    In the nighttime;
God of mine above me,
God of mine beneath me,
And the white robed angels
    Singing, "Hallelujia!"

Take me swift to Heaven,
    Singing, "Hallelujia!",
Take me swift to Heaven,
    In the nighttime;
Seat me 'mid the lilies,
Crown me with the roses,
And let white robed angels
    Sing me, "Hallelujia!"

1915

YOUTH IN HEAVEN

Frances E. W. Harper

*In heaven, the angels are advancing continually to the spring-time
of their youth, so that the oldest angel appears the youngest.*
—*Swedenborg*

Not for them the length'ning shadows,
    Falling coldly 'round our lives;
Nearer, nearer, through the ages,
    Life's new spring for them arrives. . . .

Never lines of light and darkness
    Thread the brows forever fair;
And the eldest of the angels
    Seems the youngest brother there.

There the streets of life doth never
    Cross the mournful plain of death;
And the gates of light are ever
    Closed against its icy breath.

1871

from MORNING: A PRAYER

James Mackey

Thank you, My Father, for your guardin' angel,
That guard me all night long
Until morning light appear.
And before he went from his watch,
He touch my eyes this morning with a finger of love,
And my eye become open
And behold a brand new Monday morning.

1966

PERMISSIONS

THE AUTHORS

Maya Angelou (b. 1928), a professor, poet, and autobiographer, composed "On the Pulse of Morning" for President Bill Clinton's inauguration in 1992.

Amiri Baraka (LeRoi Jones; b. 1934) is a playwright, poet, intellectual, and activist closely identified with the Black Arts movement.

Gerald Barrax (b. 1933) is a poet and professor of English at the University of North Carolina.

James Madison Bell (1826–1902), born in Ohio, was a poet, abolitionist, and politician.

Jonathan Henderson Brooks (1904–45) helped his Mississippi sharecropper parents work the fields as a child. His only book of poems was published posthumously in 1948.

Sterling Brown (1901–89), in addition to being a highly regarded poet, was a Howard University professor who held degrees from Williams and Harvard.

Margaret T. Burroughs (b. 1917), poet, artist, and art teacher, founded the DuSable Museum of African American History in Chicago.

Alfred Gibbs Campbell (?1826–?) was a devoted abolitionist who edited a newspaper in the 1850s.

James Edwin Campbell (1867–96), born in Ohio, was an educator and journalist known for skillful dialect poetry.

Noah Calwell Cannon (?1796–1850) was an AME preacher who "rode the circuit" to camp meetings throughout the eastern United States in the early 1800s.

Lucille Clifton (b. 1936), a professor, poet, children's author, and Emmy recipient, has twice been nominated for the Pulitzer Prize.

The Committee of the Colored National Convention of 1848 was composed of Frederick Douglass, H. Bibb, W. L. Day, D. H. Jenkins, and A. H. Francis. The convention movement was popular from the 1830s to 1860s.

Countee Cullen (1903–46), one of the most popular poets of the Harlem Renaissance, was also a dedicated junior high school teacher. He held degrees from NYU and Harvard.

Frederick Douglass (?1817–95), famed orator, abolitionist, autobiographer, and journalist, escaped slavery in 1838, and in 1845 published the most popular of the nineteenth-century slave narratives.

Rita Dove (b. 1952) is the second African American to win the Pulitzer Prize (for *Thomas and Beulah*, in 1987). A professor at the University of Virginia, in 1993 she was named Poet Laureate of the United States.

W. E. B. Du Bois (1868–1963), author, educator, and civil rights leader, received B.A., M.A., and Ph.D. degrees from Harvard. An early advocate of complete equality, he was one of the founders of the NAACP.

Paul Laurence Dunbar (1872–1906), poet and novelist, was the first male African-American poet to achieve both wide popularity and literary distinction. He wrote in both dialect and standard English.

First South Carolina Volunteer Regiment was the first African-American military unit of former slaves to be mustered for the Union during the Civil War.

Julia Foote (1823–1900), born in New York, was an itinerant evangelist who became the first female deacon of the AME church.

Mary Weston Fordham (?1862–?), who lived in the Carolinas, published one volume of poetry on religious and moral subjects.

Henry Highland Garnet (1815–82) was a minister and abolitionist. "A Memorial Discourse" was the first sermon delivered in the United States Congress by an African-American minister.

Charlotte L. Forten Grimke (1837–1914), teacher, poet, and abolitionist, is best known for her journals recording the day to day life of a free black woman before the Civil War.

Jupiter Hammon (1711–1806?), who lived and died a slave in New York, was known for his preaching. "Evening Thought" is the second poem known to have been written by an African American and was the first published.

Frances E. W. Harper (1825–1911) was a prominent and popular poet, novelist, abolitionist, and lecturer on women's rights, civil rights, and other social causes.

Robert Hayden (1913–80) is increasingly regarded as one of the finest American poets of his era. Many of his poems deal with the history of African-American life.

Josephine D. Heard (1861–1921) traveled widely, spending a decade in Liberia with her husband, a minister.

Joseph Cephas Holly (1825–55), a boot maker by trade, wrote passionate antislavery verse.

George Moses Horton (1797–1883?) was the first black poet to write poems of protest against slavery, and the first to have a book of poetry published in the United States.

Langston Hughes (1902–67) is perhaps the most influential African-American writer of the twentieth century. With deceptive simplicity, he uses folk and folk music traditions to speak about the black urban experience.

Zora Neale Hurston (?1901–60) studied anthropology with Frank Boas at Columbia. A popular writer of the Harlem Renaissance, she died in obscurity in a Florida county welfare home.

Harriet Jacobs (1813–97), a slave born in North Carolina, hid for seven years in a tiny attic before escaping to the North. Her autobiographical narrative was considered fictional until 1987, when it was authenticated.

John Jea (1773–?), born in Nigeria, was brought to New York as a slave. He became a sailor and preacher after being freed on the basis of his miraculous ability to read the Bible.

Fenton Johnson (1888–1958), poet, playwright, short story writer, and journalist, spent most of his life in Chicago.

James Weldon Johnson (1871–1938), poet, editor, and man of letters, authored a groundbreaking novel, *Autobiography of an Ex-Coloured Man*, in 1912. He was also a lawyer.

Martin Luther King, Jr. (1929–68) won the Nobel Peace Prize in 1963. His philosophy of nonviolent civil disobedience became the guiding principle of the early civil rights struggle in the 1950s and '60s.

Jarena Lee (1783–?), born in New Jersey, was a traveling AME evangelist (although the church did not license women to preach). Her spiritual autobiography is the earliest by an African-American woman.

James Mackey was a resident of Johns Island, South Carolina.

May Miller (b. 1899), a celebrated playwright of the Harlem Renaissance, is also a poet and children's author.

Toni Morrison (b. 1931), a widely read and critically acclaimed novelist, received the Pulitzer Prize in 1988 (for *Beloved*), and the Nobel prize in 1993.

Daniel A. Payne (1811–93), a prominent early bishop of the AME church, was also an educational leader who became the first president of a black institution of higher learning (Wilberforce University).

Ann Plato (?1820–?), of Connecticut, published a collection of moral essays, biographical sketches, and poems in 1841. Nothing more is known of her life or work.

Elymas Payson Rogers (1815–61), born in Connecticut, was an educator and ordained minister. He died while a missionary in Sierra Leone.

Ntozake Shange (b. 1948) is an award-winning feminist poet, novelist, and playwright.

Bessie Smith (1894–1937), "the Empress of the Blues," also wrote much of her own music.

Maria Stewart (1803–79), one of the earliest female political orators, was an essayist and educator who championed religious, abolitionist, and women's rights issues.

Clara Ann Thompson (1887–?) was one of three siblings who published poetry on religious and other subjects.

Phillis Wheatley (?1753–84) was brought to Boston from Africa as a slave at the age of seven. At twenty, she published *Poems on Various Subjects, Religious and Moral* (London, 1773), the first book of poetry published by an African American.

George White (b. 1764) was an itinerant Methodist evangelist and autobiographer.

James Monroe Whitfield (1822–71), born in the free North, wrote impassioned protest poetry and prose.